20 EVENTS

Disasters

THAT SHOOK THE WORLD

CATHIE CUSH

RSVP

RAINTREE
STECK-VAUGHN
PUBLISHERS
The Steck-Vaughn Company

Austin, Texas

Consultant: Gary Gerstle, Department of History, The Catholic University of America

Developed for Steck-Vaughn Company by
Visual Education Corporation, Princeton, New Jersey

Project Director: Jewel Moulthrop
Assistant Editor: Emilie McCardell
Researcher: Carol Ciaston
Photo Research: Photosearch, Inc.
Production Supervisor: Maryellen Filipek
Proofreading Management: Amy Davis
Word Processing: Cynthia C. Feldner
Interior Design: Lee Grabarczyk
Cover Design: Maxson Crandall
Page Layout: Maxson Crandall, Lisa R. Evans

Raintree Steck-Vaughn Publishers staff

Editor: Shirley Shalit
Project Manager: Joyce Spicer

Library of Congress Cataloging-in-Publication Data

Cush, Cathie, 1957–
    Disasters that shook the world / Cathie Cush
        p.   cm. — (20 Events)
    Includes bibliographical references and index.
    Summary: Describes twenty famous disasters, from the eruption of Mount Vesuvius, to the sinking of the Titanic, to Hurricanes Andrew and Iniki.
    ISBN 0-8114-4929-7
    1. Natural disasters—Juvenile literature.   2. Disasters—Juvenile literature. [1. Natural disasters. 2. Disasters.]
I. Title.   II. Series.
GB5019.C87 1994   93–10299
904—dc20   CIP
                                                     AC

Printed and bound in the United States

2 3 4 5 6 7 8 9 0   VH   99 98 97 96 95 94

Cover: Even with the ability to track developing storms by satellite pictures, some hurricanes travel too quickly to prepare for them. The inset photo shows the damage wrought by Hurricane Iniki in 1992.

Credits and Acknowledgments

Cover photos: Reuters/Bettmann (background), Reuters/Bettmann (inset)
Illustrations: American Composition and Graphics
Maps: Parrot Graphics

4: Visual Education Corporation; **5:** Visual Education Corporation; **6:** Germanisches Nationalmuseum, Nuremberg; **7:** Bibliothèque Royale Albert premier, Brussels; **8:** Peabody Museum, Harvard University; **9:** Arizona Historical Society (left), The Amerind Foundation. Photo: Robin Stancliff (right); **10:** © British Library (left), Bettmann/Hulton (right); **11:** British Tourist Authority; **12:** Linda Bartlett/Photo Researchers (left), The Bettmann Archive (right); **13:** Tony Savino/Sipa Press; **14:** Library of Congress; **15:** Chicago Historical Society (top), Garry McMichael/Photo Researchers (bottom); **17:** © Jean-Loup Charmet, Paris (left), Robert Fried/Stock Boston (right); **19:** Culver Pictures (left), Owen Franken/Stock Boston (right); **20:** The Bettmann Archive; **21:** Bettmann/Hulton; **22:** The Bettmann Archive; **23:** Alfred Pasieka/Science Photo Library/Photo Researchers (left), Andy Levin/Photo Researchers (right); **24:** Christine Osborne/Photo Researchers; **25:** UPI/Bettmann; **26:** Frilet/Sipa Press; **27:** Frilet/Sipa Press (left), Reuters/Bettmann (right); **28:** Trippett/Sipa Press; **29:** UPI/Bettmann (left), Gay Men's Health Crisis. Photo: Sharon Guynup (right); **30:** Norvan/Sipa Press (left), Mahendra/Sipa Press (right); **31:** Haley/Sipa Press; **32:** NASA; **33:** NASA (left), NASA (right); **34:** APN/Sipa Press; **35:** APN/Sipa Press (left), Sipa Press (right); **36:** Ken Graham (left), Ken Graham (right); **37:** Ken Graham (left), Nina Berman/Sipa Press (right); **38:** Visual Education Corporation; **39:** Sovfoto (left), Reuters/Bettmann (right); **41:** Wesley Bocxe/Sipa Press (left), Greenpeace/Hodson (right); **42:** Reuters/Bettmann (left), Reuters/Bettmann (right); **43:** Reuters/Bettmann

Contents

Vesuvius Explodes

A massive volcanic eruption buried intact three ancient Roman cities.

The people who lived in these ancient cities had busy lives. They often watched chariot races and gladiator contests in the public arena. They were completely unprepared for the disaster that struck on August 24.

Three Bustling Cities

About 2,000 years ago, the Roman Empire united the lands surrounding the Mediterranean Sea, northern Africa, parts of Asia, and much of western Europe. Pompeii, Stabiae, and Herculaneum were three bustling, prosperous cities in the Roman Empire. They were located at the base of Mount Vesuvius, in what is now southern Italy.

The three cities were well populated. Pompeii alone had 20,000 inhabitants. Wool processing and banking were important industries. Merchants traded wine, olive oil, and clothing. The people enjoyed attending the theater, watching gladiator contests in the public arena, and visiting with their friends in restaurants and cafés. They worshiped at temples dedicated to the Roman gods. As the residents of Pompeii, Stabiae, and Herculaneum carried out their daily activities, they never worried that the mountain looming over them might erupt. After all, Mount Vesuvius had been dormant, or inactive, for centuries.

> "The ashes began falling on us. . . . I turned my head and saw behind me a dense cloud which came rolling after us like a torrent. I suggested that while we still have light we turn off the high road, lest (my mother) be trampled to death in the dark by the crowd that followed us."
>
> —Pliny the Younger

In a letter to the historian Tacitus, Pliny recounts the details of his harrowing escape from Pompeii.

The Volcano Erupts

August 24 in A.D. 79 began like any other day in Pompeii, Stabiae, and Herculaneum. Men, women, and children got up and went about their usual routines. Then suddenly, without warning, Mount Vesuvius exploded. For two days it spewed out molten lava, red-hot cinders, and ash. Volcanic debris fell on the cities like rain, and poisonous gases filled the air. People were caught in the middle of everyday activities—cooking food, eating and drinking in cafés, bathing. As they rushed to escape the falling cinders and ash, a massive wall of mud-lava surged down the mountain and trapped them. Three-fourths of the population was killed.

Pompeii, Stabiae, and Herculaneum were completely buried. Pompeii was buried under 19 to 23 feet of lava and volcanic ash. Stabiae, farther away from the volcano, was not buried as deep as Pompeii. Herculaneum was buried under 65 feet of mud-lava.

Why Vesuvius Erupted A volcano is a vent, or opening, in the earth's crust. Through this vent, gas and rock (usually in the form of molten lava)

Lava surged down the mountainside and buried people in the midst of their daily activities. Some died from the poisonous gases. Their bodies were preserved by the ashes that engulfed them.

can be expelled from the interior of the earth.

Most volcanoes are located along the boundaries of the gigantic plates, or slabs of rock, that make up the earth's crust. The plates are constantly in motion. In some places they are forced together. When this happens, one plate slides under the neighboring plate. The movement causes a great deal of friction along the plate boundaries. The friction, in turn, melts the rock, forming highly pressurized gas and lava. These materials then escape through the deep vents of volcanoes.

Beginning in A.D. 63, a series of earthquakes indicated increasing activity below the earth's surface in the area of Mount Vesuvius. People at that time, however, did not know that earthquakes can precede volcanic eruptions. Besides the devastating eruption in A.D. 79, other major Vesuvius eruptions occurred in 1631, 1794, 1872, and 1906. Mount Vesuvius is still an active volcano, and scientists monitor it closely to detect warning signs such as increased earthquake activity.

Archaeological Treasure

The three ancient cities lay buried beneath the earth for centuries. Then, in 1709 and 1748, archaeologists discovered the long-lost ruins and began to excavate them. They were amazed at what they found. It was as if the cities had been frozen in time. Coins were still on the restaurant counters where they had been dropped. Tools for cutting gems, loaves of bread in baking ovens, and brushes for a bath lay where they had been abandoned. By pouring plaster into the hollows left by disintegrated bodies, the archaeologists were able to obtain casts of the victims.

Wall paintings and other artwork excavated at Pompeii, Stabiae, and Herculaneum fascinated 18th-century Europeans and Americans. They began to use ancient Roman designs in their architecture, art, and furniture. The famous potter Josiah Wedgwood changed the style of his work to reflect the Roman motifs.

The ruins are still being excavated today. Archaeologists have uncovered private homes and public buildings, including public baths, theaters, temples, and sports complexes. They have also uncovered inscriptions on buildings, notices of public events, and graffiti with personal messages. All of these provide an invaluable record of what life was like in the ancient Roman Empire. Even today, the ruins at Vesuvius attract the attention of tourists in southern Italy.

Archaeologists excavating the cities have provided us with invaluable knowledge of what life was like in these ancient cities.

The Black Death

A deadly disease killed one-third of the population of Europe in the 14th century.

Because of the highly contagious nature of the disease, protective clothing was worn by doctors and others who visited plague houses.

Progress and Problems

The 14th century was a time of contrasts. The world seemed smaller as explorers discovered faster routes to faraway places. Merchants from Europe began to trade with those in Asia and Africa for exotic goods. Shipping was a new industry, and ports developed along the coasts. Towns and cities grew quickly.

With the rapid growth, however, came some serious problems. People did not understand the need for sanitation to help prevent the spread of disease. They dumped raw sewage and garbage into the streets and the water. People rarely bathed. Perfumes from the Far East were popular because they masked the strong odor of unwashed bodies.

Rats also were plentiful in 14th-century Europe and Asia. They carried fleas, which in turn carried bacteria that caused a terrible disease known as the plague. This fatal illness infected both rats and humans.

Furthermore, it was highly contagious, and those infected usually died within days. Victims developed fever and other flulike symptoms. Some coughed up blood. Others developed swellings the size of small eggs on their necks and in their armpits and groins. These swollen lymph glands, called buboes, gave rise to the name *bubonic plague.* In the last stages of the illness, plague sufferers developed purple or blue-black blotches from broken blood vessels. For this reason, the disease came to be called the Black Death. Plague may have occurred as early as the 12th century B.C., but the first records of the disease describe an outbreak in Athens in 430 B.C. Another serious epidemic occurred in Rome in A.D. 262, and killed 5,000 people a day. In the 14th century, it struck again, in one of the worst epidemics of world history.

The Black Death Spreads

The outbreak may have started in 1333 in central Asia as hordes of flea-infested rats accompanied trade caravans and ships. As the rats died from the disease, the fleas infected human hosts. The plague reached the trade city of Constantinople, now Istanbul, in 1347 and quickly spread to Sicily and Greece. By the following year, it had reached France and Spain. Within a few months, people in England and Ireland were dying of bubonic plague.

In most places the pattern was the same. Urban seaports were hit first and hardest. Trade brought the disease to other towns. Then many people fled in terror to the countryside, and the Black Death followed.

One story tells of a ship from London that ran aground in a Norwegian harbor in 1349. Authorities boarded the boat and found the crew dead. When the Norwegians returned to shore, they carried with them disease-bearing fleas.

Ignorance Spreads the Disease

People of the Middle Ages didn't understand how bacteria travel. They had no idea how to prevent or treat diseases like the plague. Those who fell ill were walled up inside their own houses. Others were placed on boats and sent off to islands. People

▶ As hundreds of people died each day, many of the survivors were engaged in burying the dead. Agnolo di Tura, an Italian, wrote that he had buried his own five children with "my own hands."

huddled together out of fear. They didn't know that when they coughed or sneezed, they spread the germs that carried the Black Death. Poor sanitation made the situation worse. So did selling the clothes of the dead.

Hundreds of people dying each day created hysteria among the remaining people. They felt as though the world was coming to an end. Knowing that the Black Death could take them at any time, many people left their shops and their fields. Instead of working, they spent their days and nights eating, drinking, and dancing. Some danced in graveyards in hopes of keeping away demons. People lost their faith in the Church, which could not protect them from the epidemic. Some people joined strange new religious cults. They believed that the plague was sent to

▶ This seemingly innocent rhyme actually describes the Black Death: rosies (rash), posies (flowers to mask the odor), Achoo! (sneezing), all fall down (death).

punish sinners. Therefore, to avoid being punished in that terrible way, they whipped themselves in the streets.

During the five years in which the plague ravaged Europe, 25 million people died. This included half the total population of England and two-thirds of the student body at Oxford University. Because of the difficulty of disposing of so many dead, bodies were thrown into the rivers or heaped in communal burial pits. By doing so, they actually worsened the already poor sanitation.

Ring around the rosies,
A pocket full of posies,
Achoo! Achoo!
We all fall down.

Aftermath of the Plague

The epidemic eventually ended, but the Black Death had changed the face of Europe forever. The epidemic resulted in great economic and social changes:

- Labor shortages enabled workers to demand higher wages.
- Peasants demanded their own land.
- A shortage of teachers gave rise to the use of native languages, instead of Latin, in education.
- A shortage of priests led to splinter groups within the Church.

The survivors of the Black Death were hardy people, and the population rebounded. Outbreaks of plague still occurred, however, from time to time. The last took place in the late 19th century. It began in China and spread to Africa, Australia, the Pacific Islands, and eventually San Francisco. In 1950, the World Health Organization developed sanitation programs to help control the disease with strict quarantines and to prevent its spread with campaigns to exterminate rats. Furthermore, doctors can now treat the disease with antibiotics, so another major outbreak is unlikely. But the Black Death of the 14th century will forever be a memory of intense human suffering.

Destruction of the Native Americans

European diseases and military might nearly wiped out the New World's native peoples.

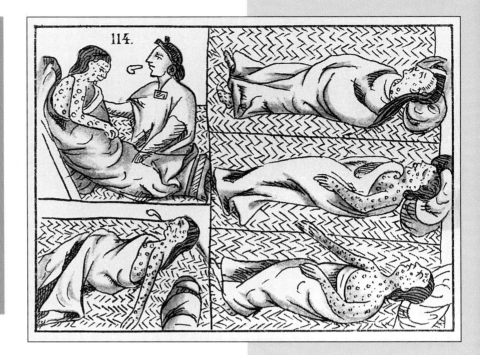

European diseases ravaged the Native Americans, who had no natural immunity against them.

Isolated Empires

Until Christopher Columbus set foot in the Americas in 1492, the inhabitants of the Western Hemisphere were isolated from the rest of the world. When the explorer landed on the islands that are now called the Bahamas, he thought he had reached the East Indies. He called the native people "Indians." That name was later applied to all the native people in the New World.

In reality, this world was not so new. The people of the Western Hemisphere had highly developed civilizations. With their great military strength, the Aztec people dominated present-day Mexico. Their capital city, Tenochtitlán, was built on islands in a lake and had between 200,000 and 300,000 inhabitants.

To the south, the Inca Empire covered more than 3,000 miles from mid-Ecuador to mid-Chile. Warrior-rulers governed from cities such as the mighty fortress Machu Picchu, high in the Andes Mountains.

In North America, independent nations were found in different geographical areas. Like the Aztecs and the Incas, these people had complex cultures, with their own art, their own religions, and their own economies. Some were farmers. Others were nomadic hunters who followed game animals through the seasons.

European Expansion Within a few years after Columbus's first voyage, other Europeans arrived in the Western Hemisphere. The Spanish sent expeditions to the Caribbean, Mexico, and South America. The British raised their flag along the coast of North America. The French, Dutch, Swedes, and Portuguese also had an interest in the New World. All these Europeans shared one belief: that they were superior to the natives. Therefore, they felt entitled to occupy Indian lands and to take Indian treasures for themselves. Few felt a need to treat the Native Americans and their cultural traditions with respect.

Clash of Cultures

The arrival of the Europeans took a terrible toll on the Native Americans. Populations were virtually wiped out in a few generations. It is difficult to determine the numbers, but experts estimate the population of central Mexico was between 15 and 25 million in 1519. By 1623, it had dropped to about 700,000. The impact was similar in other parts of the New World.

Fatal Epidemics The biggest killer of the Indian populations was disease. When the Europeans came to the New World, they brought with them the germs of all the illnesses they suffered at home. These included smallpox, measles, and typhus. Most of these illnesses were relatively harmless to the Europeans, who had been exposed to them many times and thus had built some immunity to them. The Indians, however, had no immunity to these contagious diseases. Nor did they have medications to treat them.

Although the Indians fought bravely to keep their land, they were finally defeated. Tribes were placed on isolated reservations throughout the western United States.

Within the first hundred years after the initial European contact, Indian populations were severely reduced by a series of epidemics. Perhaps the worst was a smallpox epidemic that occurred in 1519. It swept from the Caribbean through Mexico, Central America, and Peru. The disease was carried by people and by domesticated animals, such as cattle and dogs.

Gods and Guns The advanced military technology of the Europeans made them formidable conquerors. Indians had only spears and arrows. The Europeans had guns and cannon. They fought on horseback. Because horses did not exist in the New World, the Indians had never seen mounted warriors before. In some cases, they put up little resistance. They thought that these "man-beasts" were the white gods described in some of their legends. They soon learned their error. But the various Indian nations could not muster the kind of unity they needed to fight the European invasion.

The Death of the Empires

Diseases and military defeats made the Indians too weak to withstand the Europeans. Those Indians who survived were driven off their land. In Mexico and South America, the Spanish tried to enslave the once-proud Aztecs and Incas. Many tried to resist enslavement. Still, by 1600, little remained of their way of life, and their great cities fell into ruin.

Uneasy Alliances In the eastern parts of North America, Indians were pushed farther west until they clashed with the native peoples already there. In a few cases, the Indians joined the Europeans. Some Indians fought with the French against the British, and others joined the British against the American patriots during the Revolutionary War. But for the most part, they tried to fight the white invaders. In the end, however, the native people who survived ended up living in poverty on small, dilapidated reservations. By the end of the 19th century, all Native American resistance had been subdued. The descendants of the Europeans were now free to spread their culture across another continent.

Although they remained submissive for decades, Native Americans have begun to actively work for the return of their lands and for religious freedom. In the 1980s and 1990s, Indian religious leaders demanded the return of skeletal remains in museum collections. In response to these demands, the Smithsonian Institution, Stanford University, and other groups have returned Indian relics to the tribes making claims. Conflicts over land and water rights, however, still remain.

Native Americans continue to preserve their rich culture through special rites and celebrations.

9

The Great London Fire

The worst fire in the history of London raged for five furious days and burned most of the old city to the ground.

Built in the 1st century, London had grown and become an important trade center and link to Europe by the 17th century. The city consisted of narrow streets and wooden buildings crowded together.

The Old City

London in the mid-17th century was a bustling financial and trading center. The port of London was the main trade link between England and the European continent. England's richest city had a population approaching half a million.

The oldest part of London was located within the walls built by the Romans when they conquered the ancient city in A.D. 43. The area inside the walls came to be known as "the City" by Londoners. As trade increased, the walled City became dirty and overcrowded. Narrow, winding streets and alleys were tightly packed with wooden buildings topped by overhanging thatched roofs. Many people who owned ground-floor shops lived above them in dark, cramped quarters with poor sanitation.

In 1666, after a hot and dry summer, the City was a huge potential firebomb waiting to be ignited. But London was not prepared for the serious dangers of a large fire.

The Great Fire of London

The disaster began in the City on Pudding Lane near London Bridge over the Thames River. In the early morning hours on Sunday, September 2, 1666, in the house of the king's baker, a spark took hold. At first, the fire advanced slowly. Then, as a strong wind picked up, the flames quickly spread to nearby buildings. Leather water buckets and hand-held pumps were no match for this growing inferno. By the time the unrelenting wind spread the flames to Thames Street, the fire was out of control.

Warehouses by the river loaded with flammable goods and explosives fed the fierce wave of destruction. Frantic throngs of people sought safety on the river. The Thames was soon overcrowded with Londoners trying to escape by boat with their belongings. In desperation some people threw their goods in the river, hoping to retrieve them later. During the first days of the fire most Londoners appeared to be more concerned with saving their possessions than with putting out the fire.

Although the destruction of the old city was great—more than 13,000 buildings were destroyed—only a few people perished in the fire.

As the north bank of the Thames went up in flames, King Charles II sent troops to help fight the fire. He placed his brother, the duke of York, in charge. By Tuesday, the worst day of destruction, even the king and his brother had joined a bucket brigade. It was a seesaw battle in which the blaze was extinguished only to flare up again. Later that night, gunpowder was used to blow up buildings to create firebreaks, strips of cleared land, to stop the fire's relentless march. That night the wind died down, and by Wednesday the fire was contained. On Thursday, after five days of fury, the fire was out. However, the ruins continued to smolder for several months afterward.

Over three-fourths of the City was destroyed, but incredibly only six deaths were reported. The destruction included 87 churches, most of the civic buildings, over 13,000 houses, many of the buildings on London Bridge, Saint Paul's Cathedral, and the Royal Exchange. The Great Fire of London left over 200,000 people homeless.

Rebuilding the City

Within a few days after the fire, three different sets of plans for rebuilding the city were presented to the king. The king rejected plans to widen the streets and to rebuild them in the form of a grid. However, the Rebuilding Act of 1667 did ban wooden buildings and require that only stone and brick be used in reconstructing the city. The new London that rose from the ashes of the Great Fire was a much safer city with a clean new look.

Many people who were unable to wait for the city to be rebuilt moved to the growing suburbs west of the city.

In the years following the fire, England's leading architect, Sir Christopher Wren, designed over 50 churches, as well as many public and private buildings. Wren's masterpiece is the new Saint Paul's Cathedral, whose huge dome dominates London's landscape. Today, many of the buildings built after the fire are London's most treasured landmarks.

As the city was rebuilt, it expanded into the surrounding area, creating numerous suburbs. Today, London is one of the great capitals of the world.

The Irish Famine

A series of crop failures caused starvation, disease, and widespread emigration.

Ireland is called the Emerald Isle because of its lush green landscape and mild temperatures. Because of the rich pastures of its central plain, the country has long been known for its livestock.

An Unfortunate Union

In 1801, Ireland reluctantly entered into a union with Great Britain. This political and economic union, which formed the United Kingdom, took away Ireland's right to trade with foreign countries and significantly reduced the civil rights of most of the Irish people. At the time of the union, over two-thirds of the Irish population were tenant farmers, who paid a landlord rent to work the fields.

Because of their poverty, most Irish farmers in Ireland had become completely dependent on the potato crop. The typical farm family consumed about eight pounds of potatoes a day. The nutritious and fast-growing potato was planted on every inch of spare land.

In 1843, a boat from America unknowingly carried a fungus to Europe. Soon that fungus would destroy Ireland's potato crop.

Despite the famine, food and livestock were exported from Ireland to England. This political cartoon portrays the urgent cry for help from the Irish people.

The Potato Famine

The first failure of Ireland's potato crop began in 1845 and spread rapidly throughout the lush, green landscape of the Emerald Isle. The moist air and mild temperatures provided ideal conditions for the fungus to grow and spread. A fringe of white on the leaves gave the first sign that a potato plant was infected.

Ireland's potato famine is the only major recorded famine caused by a crop disease. Few potatoes from infected areas could be eaten or used as seeds for planting. Also, surplus potatoes could not be stored from one year to the next. An infected potato crop meant starvation.

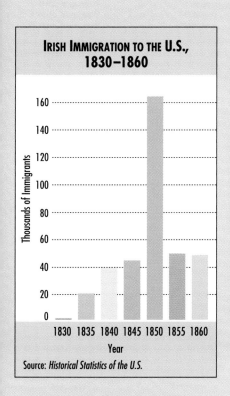

IRISH IMMIGRATION TO THE U.S., 1830–1860

Thousands of Immigrants

160
140
120
100
80
60
40
20
0

1830 1835 1840 1845 1850 1855 1860

Year

Source: *Historical Statistics of the U.S.*

Irish immigration soared during the famine years as hundreds of thousands left the country. Many came to the United States in search of a better life.

Irish cultural traditions are celebrated in many American cities. Thousands gather each year to celebrate Saint Patrick's Day. The annual parade along Fifth Avenue in New York City is shown here.

The poor harvest of 1845 caused tremendous suffering and was seen as a terrible warning of total disaster. The next year the entire potato crop rotted in the ground and filled the air with a foul smell. To make a terrible situation worse, the winter of 1846–1847 was unusually cold and bitter. The Irish starved, and disease struck the weakened people. Yet throughout the crisis, many landlords and food brokers continued to ship other food and livestock from Ireland to England.

Irish leaders found little support or help from Great Britain. British leaders were very slow to respond to what they called the "Irish problem." Aid consisted of crowding the starving poor into workhouses or feeding them in soup kitchens. And even this little help—inadequate as it was—was restricted to the poorest of the poor.

In 1847, the harvest was good, and the suffering lessened. But the potato blight returned with a vengeance in 1848. This time, starvation was accompanied by deadly outbreaks of typhus, cholera, and scurvy.

By 1849, the blight had ended. Out of an Irish population of 8 million, over 1.5 million had died. And in one of the largest emigrations in history, a million more left Ireland in search of a better life overseas. Some went to Canada or Australia, but most chose the United States.

Those Who Survived

Irish society was disrupted for a long time after the famine. The poor continued to emigrate to the United States in large numbers. Those who remained in Ireland, ever fearful of future disasters, tended to marry later and to have fewer children. Ireland's population has never again reached prefamine levels.

Among the survivors of the famine in Ireland, there remained a profound bitterness over British policies. The economic and agricultural hardships during and after the famine intensified calls for Irish self-rule among the rural poor. This large, mostly Catholic group had long been denied political power and economic opportunity by the Protestant minority ruling class.

In the United States, Irish immigrants reluctant to put their faith in farming chose to live in cities. There they faced years of prejudice and discrimination. But eventually Irish Americans became a powerful force in the economic, political, and social life of the United States.

The Great Chicago Fire

In 1871, a catastrophic fire destroyed much of the city of Chicago.

Wooden buildings and high winds contributed to the rapid spread of the fire.

Chicago's History

Chicago, Illinois, was destined to become a major city and a transportation center—a natural link between the Great Lakes and the Mississippi River. The original settlement was a cluster of traders' huts outside Fort Dearborn. With the opening of the Erie Canal in 1825, Chicago became a supply center for the westward-bound pioneers. In 1848, Chicago's first railroad began operation, assuring the continued growth of the city.

In a few years, Chicago had become the hub of ten major railroad lines. Nearly 100 trains a day came and went, serving the city's booming industries. By 1870, Chicago was the world's largest center for grain, livestock, and lumber. As the world's lumber capital, it is not surprising that the entire city—homes, stores, factories, and even streets—was built of wood.

As the city's population grew— from 4,000 to 300,000 in less than 40 years—buildings and people were crowded together. After the unusually dry summer of 1871, Chicago was like a tinderbox.

The Great Fire

Mrs. O'Leary's Cow On the evening of October 8, 1871, a fire started on the southwest side of Chicago. According to legend, the blaze started when a Mrs. Patrick O'Leary's cow kicked over a lighted oil lantern. The hay in the barn caught fire first, then the barn itself, then the neighboring buildings. Chicago is nicknamed "the Windy City," and the winds were strong that night. They quickly swept the flames through the parched city.

At the time of the fire, Chicago had no professional firefighters. The blaze raced north and east through the city with only volunteers to try to stop it. Before long, the fire was out of control. The city's tightly packed wooden buildings fueled the blaze. As the fire moved north toward the Lincoln Park neighborhood, people ran in front of it, trying to escape the flames. The fire crossed the Chicago River and consumed everything in its path. In desperation, hundreds of families jumped into the cold waters of Lake Michigan for protection.

Day of Destruction The Chicago fire burned for 24 hours before it was extinguished by much-needed rain. When the ashes cooled, four square miles—2,000 acres—had been destroyed. The fire had burned the entire downtown business district and most of the residential North Side. More than 300 people were left dead, and about 100,000 were homeless. The inferno wiped out approximately 17,000 buildings. Insurance companies estimated the property damage at more than $200 million. Fortunately, most of Chicago's stockyards and factories were saved.

Alfred R. Waud's on-the-scene sketches provide vivid glimpses of Chicago's worst disaster.

Some of the most noted architects were attracted to the rebuilding of the city. Chicago is well known for its innovative and exciting architecture.

Reconstructing Chicago

Rebuilding the devastated city began almost immediately. City leaders had learned from past mistakes. This time the city would be built of stone. Strict building codes, including fireproofing, would help prevent another disaster. A professional fire department was also established, with firefighters specially trained to deal with future fires.

The rebuilding of Chicago attracted some of the nation's best architects. The modern urban center they created became known for its striking buildings. William Le Baron Jenney designed and built the world's first metal-frame skyscraper in Chicago. His ten-story Home Insurance Building was completed in 1885 and began a new trend in urban architecture. Other noted architects who left their marks on the Chicago skyline included Louis Sullivan, Daniel H. Burnham, John W. Root, and Dankmar Adler. Today, the city is still well-known for its soaring skyscrapers and striking architectural achievements, including the Sears Tower and the John Hancock Center.

Krakatoa's Eruption

One of the most catastrophic eruptions in history was heard thousands of miles away.

A Small Uninhabited Island

Volcanoes are dramatic and terrifying natural events. Compressed heat at the center of the earth breaks through the earth's crust, sending huge amounts of fire, smoke, and sound into the atmosphere. One of the most spectacular volcanic eruptions in history occurred on a small uninhabited island in the Indian Ocean.

Krakatoa is located among the islands of Indonesia, between Java and Sumatra. This volcanic island was formed sometime within the last one million years. Over the centuries, three smaller volcanic cones merged to become this one island. By the 19th century, Krakatoa was 7 miles long and 4 miles wide, with a landmass of about 28 square miles. The tallest of its three volcanic peaks rose 2,667 feet above sea level.

In 1680, one of the cones produced a moderate eruption. There was no volcanic activity for the next two centuries. But on May 20, 1883, one of the smaller cones erupted. A German sea captain reported a cloud of vapor and ash that rose 6 miles above the palm-covered island. More activity was reported on June 19 and through that summer. By August 26, the ash cloud was 17 miles high.

Krakatoa Explodes

At 10 A.M. on August 27, 1883, Krakatoa was rocked by one of the most catastrophic volcanic eruptions in history. The pressure that had been building beneath the earth's crust could no longer be contained. A series of four explosions blew ash and debris for miles. The third explosion alone released force equal to 200 megatons of TNT.

Krakatoa's eruption created the loudest sound in recorded history. People living as far away as the Philippines, Western Australia, and India—all nearly 2,000 miles from the source of the explosion—heard the noise. Four hours after the eruption occurred, its thunderous roar was heard by people on the island of Rodrigues, some 3,000 miles on the other side of the Indian Ocean. That is like people living in New York being able to hear an explosion in California. Like most volcanic eruptions, this one also produced a shock wave. However, the force of the eruption was so great that the shock wave traveled around the earth seven times!

Year	Volcano	Estimated Casualties	Principal Cause of Death
1631	Vesuvius (Italy)	18,000	Lava flows, mudflows
1783	Laki (Iceland)	10,000	Lava flows, volcanic gas, starvation
1815	Tambora (Indonesia)	92,000	Starvation
1883	Krakatoa (Indonesia)	36,000	Tidal waves
1902	Mont Pelée, Martinique (West Indies)	36,000	Gaseous clouds
1980	Mount St. Helens (U.S.A.)	57	Lateral blast, mudflows
1982	El Chicón (Mexico)	2,000	Explosions, gaseous clouds
1985	Nevado del Ruiz (Colombia)	25,000	Mudflows
1991	Pinatubo (Philippines)	300	Mudflows, gaseous clouds, ash fall

VOLCANIC ERUPTIONS, 1631–1991

Ash falls from volcanic eruptions destroy vegetation and cause respiratory problems. Mudflows are especially deadly since they are very fast and impossible to stop or divert. The most deadly and destructive of volcanic features is the glowing cloud of superheated gases, steam, and incandescent powdery lava—nearly as thick as a liquid—that flows down the slope at speeds of up to 300 miles per hour. And in some instances, such as Tambora in 1815, there is the starvation that results from the destruction of all food sources.

Black Sky When Krakatoa erupted, 5 cubic miles of ash, lava, and red-hot boulders shot into the air. Rocks flew for miles. Ash rose 50 miles and covered everything in sight. It fell over 300,000 square miles—an area about three times the size of Colorado. On nearby islands, the ash and pumice fragments were 200 feet deep. At midday, the sky above the nearby cities was as dark as midnight. It stayed that way for nearly three days.

Wall of Water After molten rock was released, the cones collapsed on themselves. They left a huge crater 5 miles wide and 900 feet deep. The collapsing cones created an underwater shock wave, called a tsunami. This tidal wave, estimated at 120 feet high, sent billions of tons of water toward the low-lying coasts of nearby islands. The wave destroyed 165 villages on Java and Sumatra and killed more than 36,000 people. Ships in the Sunda Strait, between the two islands, disappeared. Smaller islands were covered with water. As the great underwater shock wave traveled, the sea level rose even in the English Channel, half a world away.

The eruptions continued, getting smaller and less violent throughout the day. By the morning of August 28, Krakatoa was quiet. All that remained was a single small peak.

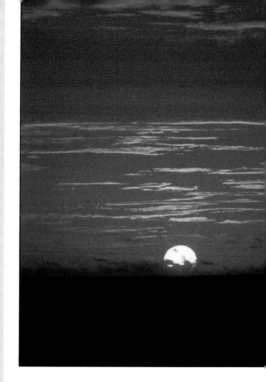

Changes in the sunsets provided scientists with valuable information about air currents in the upper atmosphere.

In the Aftermath

Fine dust particles were blasted high into the upper layers of the atmosphere. They circled the globe for a year, reducing the amount of sunlight that reached the earth by 13 percent. Sunlight reflecting off these dust particles created spectacular sunrises and sunsets for more than a year after the eruption. The sunsets were so extraordinary that on October 30, people in New York and Connecticut pulled fire alarms, mistaking the brilliant red glow in the west for fire. The dust also gave scientists the first evidence of air currents in the upper atmosphere.

Small eruptions continued to occur through February 1884. Then Krakatoa became still. But on December 29, 1927, the volcano erupted again. Within a month, a new cone had formed a small island. Called Anak Krakatoa, meaning "child of Krakatoa," the new peak is now nearly 700 feet above sea level.

Most of the damage from the Krakatoa eruption was the result of what happened beneath the water's surface. The force of the explosion triggered an underwater shock wave that sent billions of tons of water toward neighboring coastlines.

The San Francisco Earthquake (1906)

An earthquake rocked
San Francisco for 48 seconds,
toppling buildings and igniting fires
that ravaged the city
for three days.

San Francisco at the Turn of the Century

The discovery of gold in California in 1849 turned San Francisco into a boom town. Hoping to make a quick fortune, hordes of people rushed to the city. There they crowded into hastily constructed housing. The city became the main center of supplies and recreation for miners. Gradually, wetlands and part of the bay were filled in to make room for new housing.

As the gold ran out, San Francisco became a center for trade. Even before the completion of the transcontinental railroad in 1869, the port city was known as the "gateway to the Orient." By the turn of the century, San Francisco had become a world-class commercial and financial center. This once "rough-and-tumble" town had gained a reputation as a city of style and culture. In 1906, 350,000 people lived in San Francisco.

San Francisco is located near a long fracture, or break, in the earth's crust. This fracture is called the San Andreas Fault. Faults occur when two landforms, called plates, rub together in opposite directions. Sudden movements along faults result in earthquakes.

Earthquake Rocks the Sleeping City

At 5:13 A.M. on April 18, 1906, most San Franciscans were asleep. Suddenly, the plates along the San Andreas Fault shifted and a severe earthquake rocked the city. It hit without warning and lasted 48 seconds.

Buildings swayed and many collapsed. Bricks and masonry rained into the street. Power lines snapped. Huge cracks opened in the streets and alleys, gas pipes leaked, and water pipes ruptured. Overturned stoves spilled their hot coals, igniting electrical sparks and escaping gas. Fires shot up everywhere.

In the first half hour after the quake, over 50 fires raged throughout the city. Firefighters struggled to put out the fires but couldn't—the city's water main, built directly across the fault, had broken. Many separate fires soon became one blazing inferno. Only along the waterfront could firefighters make a difference. There they pumped seawater and, with the help of navy fireboats, were able to protect the docks that were San Francisco's lifeline.

Plates along a fault may move in three different ways: up and down, back and forth, or a combination of the two.

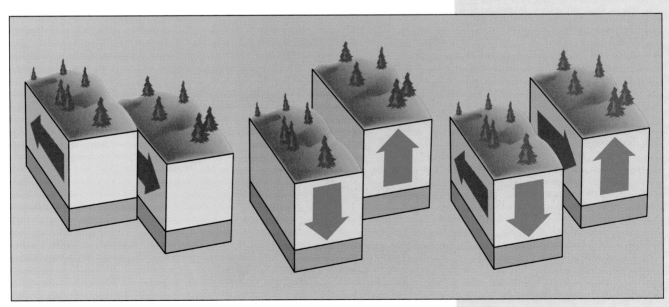

In the western part of the city, the army used cannons, dynamite, and other explosives to blow up buildings along Van Ness Avenue. They did this to create a firebreak, a strip of cleared land made to halt the spreading flames. Once the fire was contained, all people could do was watch helplessly from the hills as the city burned. The fire burned for three long days and nights.

When the smoke cleared, no exact count of the dead could be made. Varying estimates suggest that—

- 500 people died.
- 350 people were declared missing and never found.
- 400 were seriously injured.
- 250,000 were left homeless.

The heart of the city was a smoldering ruin. More than 28,000 buildings within a 4.5-square-mile area were completely destroyed. The entire business district was demolished. The parts of the city built on landfill suffered the worst destruction. Much more damage was caused by the fire than by the earthquake itself.

Scientists use the history of previous earthquakes to predict how often a region may expect a quake. They predict that an earthquake larger than the 1906 and 1989 quakes will occur in the future. This photograph shows San Francisco today.

Rebuilding San Francisco

San Franciscans were courageous despite the destruction of their city. Almost immediately, crews began clearing the debris. The work continued round the clock—24 hours a day, seven days a week. Most of the rubble was dumped into the shallows of the bay. Within two months, builders had constructed more than 8,000 simple wooden barracks, which housed up to eight families each.

A year after the quake, almost all of the rubble was gone. Construction boomed; over 20,000 new houses were built by the end of the third year.

Earthquakes frequently occur in California—as many as 40,000 a year—but only about 10 percent of these are strong enough to be felt at all. One of the strongest quakes ever recorded in the state struck northern California in 1989. On October 17, minutes before the start of the third game of the World Series between the San Francisco Giants and the Oakland Athletics, an earthquake hit the bay area. The game was canceled and 58,000 people were evacuated from Candlestick Park. Today, cities from San Francisco to Santa Cruz—a distance of about 75 miles—are still recovering from the 1989 earthquake.

Buildings collapsed and huge cracks opened in the streets, but most of the damage was caused by the fires that followed the earthquake.

The Sinking of the *Titanic*

The "unsinkable" luxury liner hit an iceberg and sank with 1,500 people on board.

The Best Ever

When the British luxury liner R.M.S. *Titanic* was ready to make its first voyage in 1912, people said the ship was unsinkable. The ship's hull had a double bottom and 16 watertight compartments designed to keep it floating even if the hull was breached. The vessel also carried a new invention, the wireless radio, which could be used to call for help at sea. The largest, most elegant ocean liner of its day, the *Titanic* was like a floating city. Passengers could eat at four restaurants, enjoy plays in the theater, relax in the Turkish bath, and play tennis, squash, and miniature golf. The ship even had a kennel for pets.

About 1,300 passengers and 890 crew members were on board on April 12, 1912, when the *Titanic* left Southampton, England, for New York on its first voyage. Passengers included well-known millionaires and poor immigrants. The band played as the ship left the dock. Eager to set a new speed record, Captain Edward J. Smith ignored several warnings that he received about icebergs in the shipping lanes and chose not to post additional lookouts.

A Night to Remember

The dark, moonless night of April 14 found the *Titanic* in the North Atlantic, about 400 miles southeast of Newfoundland. At about 11:35 P.M., a crewman spotted a dark mass off the starboard, or right, side of the ship. Grabbing the phone to the bridge, he shouted, "Iceberg dead ahead!" The first officer did not hesitate. He turned the wheel sharply, then held his breath and waited. Moments later, the crew felt a bump and heard a terrible scraping sound. The ocean started to pour into several of the watertight compartments where the ship had hit the iceberg. As the ship filled with water and became heavier, it began to tilt to one side.

Women and Children First About an hour later, Captain Smith ordered women and children into the lifeboats. Because lifeboat procedures had never been rehearsed, chaos followed. Still believing that the *Titanic* was unsinkable, many passengers ignored the order. Others tried to board the lifeboats but soon found that there weren't enough. In the

Inadequate preparation and the lack of rescue equipment resulted in the deaths of 1,500 people.

People waited anxiously for news of relatives and friends who had been on the *Titanic*. Of the 1,500 who perished, about 156 were women and children.

confusion, the crew launched many lifeboats before they were full. As the danger became frighteningly clear, the ship's wireless operator radioed frantically for help. But no one responded. The *Californian,* less than ten miles away, did not hear the signal, because the ship's wireless operator had gone off duty and had turned off the radio. The crew on the *Californian* spotted flares coming from the vicinity of the *Titanic* but did not recognize them as distress signals.

An Icy Grave Almost 60 miles away, one ship did hear the *Titanic*'s urgent call for help. The liner *Carpathia* headed for the sinking ship, but arrived too late. At 2:20 A.M. on April 15, the "unsinkable" *Titanic* stood on end, then slipped beneath the surface of the sea. Those in the lifeboats watched in horror as the ship disappeared, taking about 1,500 people to the bottom. When the *Carpathia* arrived two hours later, the only sign of the *Titanic* was its lifeboats. The *Carpathia* picked up around 700 survivors and took them to safety in New York.

What Went Wrong

Reforms for Safety About six weeks after the tragedy, a British court found the *Titanic*'s owners, the White Star Line, guilty of negligence. The ship had carried only enough lifeboats for about one-third of the people on board. Furthermore, the passengers and crew had not been informed of their proper use.

To prevent another similar disaster, the first International Convention for Safety of Life at Sea met in London in 1913. It ruled that ships must have lifeboat space for everyone aboard and that lifeboat drills must be held on every voyage. It also required that ships keep their radio on with a crew member present around the clock. In addition, the International Ice Patrol was formed to alert vessels to the presence of icebergs in the North Atlantic shipping lanes. As safety regulations were adopted internationally, many countries established special agencies to enforce them.

Lost—and Found On September 1, 1985, a team of American and French scientists, led by Dr. Robert Ballard, located the remains of the *Titanic* about two and a half miles beneath the surface. Using submersible robots and cameras, the oceanographers captured images of the ghostly wreck. The *Titanic* had broken in two when it sank. The front section still sat upright and intact, as if it were cruising along a sea of sand. The rear was a jumble of debris. The scientists photographed such items as champagne bottles, serving dishes, china, and even a child's doll.

The team also solved the mystery of why the ship had sunk. An iceberg had not cut a 300-foot gash in the side of the ocean liner, as many people had believed. Instead, some of the hull plates had buckled and rivets that joined the seams had come loose. As a result, the compartments flooded, and the *Titanic* and those still aboard went down to a watery grave.

" . . . I jumped out feet first.

I was clear of the ship, went down and as I came up I was pushed away from the ship by some force. I came up facing the ship and one of the funnels seemed to be lifted off and fell toward me . . .

I saw the ship in a sort of red glare . . . At this time I was sucked down . . . and twisted around by a large wave, coming up in the midst of a great deal of wreckage."

J. B. Thayer, Jr., a 17-year-old student from Haverford, Pennsylvania, told the story of his escape.

World Flu Epidemic

A worldwide epidemic resulted in more than 20 million deaths in two years.

Fatal Epidemic

Influenza, often called flu, is a common disease. But every 50 years or so, major outbreaks of flu strike many people throughout the world at the same time. Since the 16th century, when the flu was first identified, the world has experienced 31 epidemics of influenza.

Still, as recently as the beginning of the 20th century, very little was known about the cause of influenza or how to control it. Along with pneumonia and tuberculosis, influenza killed 300,000 people a year in the United States alone at the turn of the century. Those who lived cramped together in crowded city tenements, where germs could spread easily, were hit hardest.

Chills That Kill Today we know that influenza is caused by a virus. The virus spreads from person to person through the air, traveling on droplets of moisture from coughs and sneezes. When inhaled, the virus comes in contact with cells in the upper respiratory system and begins to reproduce. New flu viruses are released from the infected cells and spread to other cells in the lungs and in other parts of the body.

The flu itself will usually end in a week or so. People weakened by flu, however, generally have lower resistance to other diseases. Therefore, they are at greater risk of being struck by another, more serious disease, such as pneumonia. If one of these infections strikes a weakened flu patient, the results can sometimes be fatal.

While the world was at war, the worst flu epidemic in history occurred. It lasted about two years—from 1917 to 1919—and killed more than 20 million people around the globe.

The virus spread from person to person through the air. People wore gauze masks to keep from inhaling the virus.

This is one type of flu virus. The spikes help the virus attach itself to host cells. Once attached, the virus begins to reproduce. The new viruses then spread to other cells.

At War with Disease

The epidemic started with two small outbreaks of flu in 1916 and in 1917. On March 11, 1918, a soldier at Fort Riley, Kansas, reported sick. He complained of fever, sore throat, headache, and aching muscles. By noon that same day, 109 people had been admitted to the hospital with the same symptoms. By the end of the week, Fort Riley had 522 cases, and reports of other cases came in from military camps across the country. American troops may have carried the disease overseas.

No Boundaries A second wave of flu hit a few months later. In August, health authorities in Asia and Europe reported cases of the disease. By October it covered the map, even wiping out remote Eskimo villages. In India, more people died in two months from flu and accompanying infections than had died from cholera in the previous 20 years. So many died there in so short a time that it was impossible to count the casualties accurately. On the battlefields of Europe, where soldiers had been weakened by years of trench warfare, flu spread wildly. Overall, the flu epidemic resulted in 10 million more deaths than the fighting of World War I.

Impact in the United States This second wave struck the United States at the end of August 1918. A sailor in Boston complained of flu symptoms. It spread through New England, then along the East Coast. In a panic, people closed public buildings—theaters, schools, and even churches—and wore protective masks. Fines were levied for spitting in public and for coughing or sneezing without a handkerchief. More than 13,000 people died in Philadelphia, the hardest-hit American city. One Philadelphia priest searched the slums for victims and recovered more than 200 bodies in a single day. Approximately 21,000 Americans died in the last week of October. It was the highest seven-day mortality rate in U.S. history.

Illness Leads to Answers

By studying blood samples from people who survived the 1917–1919 epidemic, doctors identified the virus that caused the epidemic. In the 1940s, they discovered that vaccines, which use dead or weakened strains of the virus, can help prevent the illness in some people. The virus changes so rapidly, scientists must recreate the flu vaccine each year, based on their best guess of what the new virus will be like.

Although doctors still can't cure the flu, they can treat the symptoms with medication. More important, today they can use penicillin and other antibiotics to cure the secondary infections that may follow the illness. Although flu epidemics occurred again in 1957 and in 1968, neither of these had the impact of the influenza epidemic of 1917–1919.

Doctors use the newly created vaccine to inoculate mostly children and the elderly—two groups that are especially vulnerable to flu.

The Bangladesh Cyclone (1970)

A cyclone ripped through Bangladesh and killed hundreds of thousands.

Crowded seacoast villages like this one were hardest hit, as tides reached 15 feet higher than normal.

Formerly East Pakistan

The Bay of Bengal is a pyramid-shaped body of water between India and Southeast Asia. At its tip lies Bangladesh, formerly East Pakistan. The Bay of Bengal is the site of some of the world's fiercest storms. Called cyclones, these storms start over the warm waters of the Indian Ocean. They are funneled into the Bay of Bengal, where their force is concentrated as they approach the delta of the Ganges River. In 1963, one of these cyclones killed 20,000 people who lived along the Ganges delta. In 1965, two severe storms struck East Pakistan, killing about 40,000 people.

East Versus West From 1948 until 1971, the government and economy of East Pakistan were controlled by West Pakistan, which is 1,000 miles away. The people of East Pakistan were very poor. Most were packed tightly on low-lying islands along the coast, where they could barely raise enough rice or catch enough fish to feed themselves. The country did not have radar systems that could warn of approaching storms or any plans for dealing with storm emergencies.

Cyclone Hits in 1970

In November 1970, a cyclone developed in the southern Bay of Bengal. Its winds increased in strength as the storm traveled north. As it moved, the storm pushed water ahead of itself, forming giant waves. Its winds reached over 100 miles per hour.

Just after midnight on November 13 the center of the storm struck the Ganges delta. At high tide, the coastal islands were hit with waves 10 to 15 feet higher than normal. One wave was estimated to be 50 feet high. Water covered the islands, many of which were only a few feet above sea level. The bamboo houses on the islands could not withstand the winds and waves. On Manpura Island, only 4 of the 4,500 bamboo dwellings remained standing after the storm. Entire villages vanished.

More than a million acres of rice paddies disappeared. One million head of livestock drowned. Fishing boats were hurled inland or lost to the sea.

The Human Cost Most devastating were the human losses. People held tightly to the tops of palm trees. They watched in horror while their families and friends, unable to hold on any longer, drowned in the rushing water. The official death toll was between 200,000 and 500,000 people, but losses probably were much higher. In Manpura alone, at least 25,000 of the 30,000 people died in the storm. The largest island, Bhola, lost 200,000 people—about one-fifth of its population. On the 13 small islands off the city of Chittagong, no one survived the terrible waves. In terms of loss of human life, it was the worst storm in history.

The Waters Recede

The pain and suffering did not end with the storm. When the storm passed, the survivors were left to deal with the dead. Bodies by the thousands washed ashore with the tides. The living wore scarves around their faces to protect themselves from the terrible smell of death that was everywhere. No matter how hard the survivors worked, more bodies remained. One mass grave held 5,000 victims of the storm. Corpses were piled on rafts and sent out to sea. But when the tide came in, it brought them back to shore.

Soon those still living began to die. Some died of injuries sustained during the storm. Without food, fresh water, or medicine, many more people died of starvation or illness. Tens of thousands of refugees left East Pakistan for India.

Slow to Respond The government of West Pakistan was slow to send help—and when they did, it was too little. Grain sat in government warehouses for days before it was shipped to East Pakistan. Forty government helicopters remained on the ground in West Pakistan while the East Pakistanis waited for help.

The rest of the world tried to help. The Red Cross shipped food, clothing, and medicine to the disaster area. People were vaccinated to prevent the spread of cholera, a deadly disease. Parcels of rice were dropped from the air to feed the hungry people. In all, East Pakistan received about $50 million in foreign donations after the storm.

Another Storm The people of East Pakistan resented the inadequate help from the government in West Pakistan. In the storm-battered region, people were angry and talked of independence. Then, on March 26, 1971, the East Pakistanis declared their independence from West Pakistan. They formed a new nation called Bangladesh.

Although their government had changed, the people of the Ganges delta were still defenseless against future storms. Plans for storm-warning systems, better communications, and the construction of storm refuges never materialized. Bans on living along the coast failed. Too many people wanted to live on this fertile farmland despite the risk. To this day, the people of Bangladesh remain highly vulnerable to cyclones.

Survivors of the tidal wave gather grain in the wake of the cyclone. Difficulties in removing dead bodies led to serious health problems for the people of Bangladesh.

Famine in Ethiopia and Somalia

✦

Drought-induced famine and civil war brought misery and suffering to millions in Africa.

Emerging Nations

In the late 19th century, the nations of Europe established colonies in Africa and imposed their political systems on the African people. In the mid-20th century, strong feelings of African nationalism emerged. In the 1960s, many African countries won their independence from their European rulers.

For most people in these countries, however, life did not improve. A number of factors worked against them. The new governments tried too hard to industrialize their economies, often at the expense of agricultural programs. In doing so, they badly disrupted the economy.

In some cases, the new governments themselves were a problem. There were many corrupt leaders who used their positions to enrich themselves and their supporters. Ethnic conflict within African nations increased as different tribes fought each other for control of the government. The emerging nations depended heavily on foreign aid to support their economies. But international politics proved harmful, too. During the Cold War, the United States and the Soviet Union proved too willing to offer arms to potential African allies. Sometimes they backed different groups within the same nation, thereby encouraging the spread of civil wars. When, in the 1980s, the superpowers reduced much of their monetary support to Africa, various ethnic groups in countries like Ethiopia and Somalia continued to fight among themselves. These civil wars destroyed crops and made it difficult to transport food to areas that needed it.

Weather patterns and farming practices contributed to the problem as well. Famine is not new to this region. Since the 16th century, Ethiopia has suffered a serious food shortage about every 11 years, when drought struck large sections of the African continent. When it did rain, the torrents of water eroded the soil. Farmers overworked the thin layer of topsoil that remained. As forests were cut down for lumber and firewood, valuable nutrients were lost from the soil. Livestock grazed on and trampled already sparse vegetation. As a result, many areas of Africa on the edge of the Sahara Desert were turning into deserts themselves. At the same time, the population was increasing. This further strained food resources.

Misuse of the land and years of drought turned many areas into desert, making agriculture impossible.

Famine!

These ongoing problems resulted in recurring famine in sub-Saharan Africa. About 2 million Ethiopians starved to death in 1984 and 1985. In all, 7.5 million suffered from malnutrition. People walked for miles from their villages to the refugee camps. Some died on the way. Others were too weak to survive once they had made the journey. Diseases such as dysentery, typhoid, hepatitis, and cholera swept through the crowded refugee camps. Entire families perished. Their emaciated bodies were wrapped in rags and buried in mass graves.

The world paid little attention to the problem until October 23, 1984, when the British Broadcasting Corporation showed a seven-minute film depicting the horror of mass starvation in two towns in northern Ethiopia. Soon the suffering became well known. Through newspapers, magazines, and television, the world saw pictures of gaunt children who looked like walking skeletons with large, dark, sad eyes.

Civil war prevented much of the food from being delivered to the starving people waiting in refugee camps.

Starvation in Somalia In 1992, famine struck Somalia, a desert nation to the east of Ethiopia. By autumn, approximately 150,000 people had died and 1.8 million—nearly one-third of the population—were starving. The tragedy of famine was made worse in Somalia by civil war. Bloody fighting and looting forced more than 2 million people from their rural homes. This also ended most possible agricultural activity. As many as 200 people a day poured into refugee camps. Relief workers mixed batches of corn, beans, and vegetable oil in large drums to feed the starving people. Very young children received protein biscuits. Still, there wasn't enough to feed everyone who waited at the gates for a meal. To make matters worse, warring factions stole much of the food before it could reach the camps.

Global Response to Hunger

The suffering in Africa was overwhelming. Some people said that too little help was sent, or that it was sent too late. But many nations around the world did contribute food and aid. In December 1984, a group of rock stars released "Do They Know It's Christmas?" The hit record raised millions of dollars for famine relief. The following summer, singer Bob Geldof organized Live Aid, a huge concert staged simultaneously in London and Philadelphia to raise money for additional famine relief.

The Red Cross mounted the largest relief effort in its history, sending more than $100 million in food and aid to Somalia. However, civil war and logistical problems prevented the supplies from getting through. In December 1992, under a mandate from the United Nations, the United States, France, and other nations sent more than 28,000 troops to Somalia to protect the delivery of relief supplies to the stricken regions.

In 1992, the United Nations sent troops to Somalia to ensure the delivery of food and other relief supplies to the stricken areas.

27

The AIDS Epidemic

A disease discovered in the 1980s becomes a modern-day plague.

A New and Deadly Disease

In 1981, doctors noticed a new trend. They saw a number of cases of rare disorders, including a kind of pneumonia and a form of cancer. These diseases occurred in otherwise healthy young men who were homosexuals. Doctors also saw the diseases in people who used intravenous drugs and in Haitians.

Within a few months, public health officials realized that they were faced with a new infectious disease. They called it acquired immune deficiency syndrome, or AIDS. The disease weakened the immune system, the body's defense against disease.

Fear and misunderstanding regarding AIDS soon mounted. Some claimed that AIDS was God's way of punishing drug users and homosexuals. People thought they could catch AIDS through casual contact, such as sneezing or touching. Many people with the disease were fired from their jobs and discriminated against in other ways. Infected children were isolated or told to leave school.

The Virus Takes Hold

Trail of a Virus As the number of cases spread, researchers focused on trying to understand the disease. Scientists in the United States and France found that AIDS is caused by a virus, which they named HIV, or human immunodeficiency virus. HIV enters the body's cells and weakens the immune system, leaving the person open to one or more opportunistic diseases such as pneumonia and the unusual cancer that had first been noticed.

Researchers also learned that the virus is passed from person to person through certain body fluids. They identified four ways in which the virus could be transmitted:

- By sexual contact with an HIV-infected person
- By sharing needles with an infected person
- By getting a transfusion of infected blood
- By an infected pregnant woman passing the disease to her baby.

The researchers also found that a person could be infected with HIV for years before AIDS developed. But once a person had AIDS, he or she usually died in two to three years.

This quilt, made of tens of thousands of individual panels, memorializes those who died of AIDS. The traveling display is used to increase awareness and raise funds to support AIDS patients.

The Disease Spreads It didn't take long for HIV to reach epidemic proportions. Between 1981 and 1985, 10,000 people in the United States had developed AIDS. In the next four years, that number increased tenfold. By January 1992, more than 200,000 Americans had AIDS, and 120,000 people had died. Furthermore, between 1 million and 1.5 million people had been infected with HIV. As time went on, AIDS struck people from all walks of life—men, women, and children; rich and poor; ordinary people and celebrities.

Although AIDS was first diagnosed in New York and California, it is a global disease. It has run rampant in Africa and Asia and has spread to Latin America. Public health officials estimate that by the turn of the century, 10 million people around the world will have AIDS.

Fifteen-year-old Ryan White contracted AIDS from a transfusion. He was barred from school until he obtained a health certificate from local officials. More information about the disease will prevent discrimination against those who have it.

As the disease spread to all segments of the population, more people became involved in calling for action.

Fighting AIDS

By the early 1990s, researchers still had not found a cure for HIV infection. The only effective cure is prevention. Education is the best weapon against the spread of the disease. Public health officials urged avoiding sexual contact, using "safe sex" practices, and not sharing needles. These measures apparently have helped reduce the number of new AIDS cases. Blood banks developed methods for screening donated blood for HIV to prevent it being passed in transfusions. A change in attitudes is taking place, too. As HIV infects more people, and as people learn more about the disease, they become more sympathetic to those with the disease. State and federal laws protect people with AIDS against discrimination. Many celebrities joined in the effort to protect people with AIDS and to promote research for a cure. Serious problems remain, however. Many AIDS victims cannot get health insurance, and people are still being fired if they have AIDS.

New Drugs While they haven't found a cure, researchers have discovered drugs that will delay the onset of AIDS. One drug, called AZT, slows the progression of AIDS in people who have HIV. However, AZT has some serious side effects. Antibiotics, radiation, and other therapies are used to treat some symptoms. But so far, there is no way to prevent people with AIDS from dying of the disease. Some experimental drugs are being developed and tested to cure the disease.

AIDS activists are not content with slow progress in the face of the epidemic. They have fought successfully to have some experimental drugs put on the market quickly. Still, it will probably be many years before an effective vaccine or treatment for AIDS is found.

Bhopal Chemical Disaster

❖

The worst industrial accident in history resulted in the deaths of 3,500 people in India.

People and animals were struck down where they stood. There was no time or place to escape.

Large corporations are encouraged to build facilities in areas like Bhopal because they create jobs for the people who live there.

In a Crowded Neighborhood

In the 1970s, the Union Carbide Corporation built a chemical plant on the outskirts of Bhopal in central India. At the time, Bhopal was a growing city of about 700,000 people. The plant was located near the city's densely populated slums and shantytowns. Bhopal's leaders welcomed the plant and the jobs it created, just as they had welcomed other types of industry.

But few of the people living near the plant understood the dangers that the plant represented. The chemicals it manufactured were deadly poisons used to control agricultural pests. Nor did they know that no emergency plans existed to protect them in case of a serious accident at the plant. In fact, the plant had experienced six small accidents in its seven years of operation.

The Night of Death

On the evening of December 2, 1984, heat and pressure began to build in a storage tank. The tank contained methyl isocyanate (MIC), a chemical used in pesticides. A worker, noticing the high pressure reading on a gauge, called a supervisor around 11 P.M. But it was too late. The pressure was already too high to control. At 12:56 A.M. a faulty valve ruptured, and the chemical escaped into the air. It formed a huge cloud of deadly vapor that drifted over the sleeping city.

Two safety systems at the plant should have prevented the problem. The first was a scrubber that should have neutralized the highly toxic gas by combining it with another chemical. The scrubber either failed or could not process the amount of gas that was leaking from the storage tank. Another device, which would have burned the gas before it could do any harm to people or animals, also failed.

The Nightmare As the deadly poison drifted over the city, the people of Bhopal lived a nightmare. Asleep in their beds, many people died without ever knowing what had happened. Others, blinded by the poison, tried to run away. After inhaling the poison, they gasped for breath and coughed up blood. There was no escape from the deadly black cloud. The results were disastrous:

- Poison claimed 3,500 lives.
- More than 20,000 others suffered blindness or damage to their liver or intestines.
- The poison affected some people's lungs and nervous systems.
- Pregnant women miscarried and babies were stillborn.

By the end of the week, overcrowded hospitals and clinics treated about 150,000 people. Medical facilities were overwhelmed. They didn't have enough oxygen or antibiotics to treat the sick. In many cases, the doctors themselves were too ill to treat other victims.

Severe Criticism

In the wake of the accident, people criticized large multinational corporations like Union Carbide. Critics accused these companies of taking advantage of loose safety regulations in Third World countries. Union Carbide denied that this was the case. Company officials claimed that the safety procedures at the Bhopal plant were identical to those at its sister plant in Institute, West Virginia. The West Virginia plant, however, had a computerized warning system that the Bhopal plant didn't have. Later in the week, the chairman of Union Carbide, Warren Anderson, flew to Bhopal to inspect the damage. He was arrested when he landed and was charged with criminal and corporate negligence. Authorities released him that day, but maintained that the accident was a result of negligence. Investigations proved that the plant at Bhopal did not have the safety systems that it should have had. After five years of negotiations, the chemical company agreed to pay $470 million in compensation to the heirs of adult victims.

Safety in the Balance The chemical disaster at Bhopal highlighted a conflict that has become common in today's world. Local governments want to attract industry to densely populated areas because plants provide jobs for the people who live there. But many types of plants pose danger to those who live near them.

In 1983, the Indian government had planned to ban hazardous industry in densely populated areas, but no action was taken at the time. After the Bhopal disaster, the Indian government promised to enact stricter safety guidelines. But for thousands of people, the promises came too late.

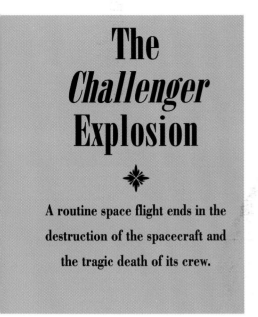

The *Challenger* Explosion

✦

A routine space flight ends in the destruction of the spacecraft and the tragic death of its crew.

This photo, taken two months before the fatal explosion, shows the *Challenger* crew. Crew members are (*back row, left to right*) Astronauts Ellison S. Onizuka, Christa McAuliffe, Gregory Jarvis, Judith A. Resnick, (*front row*) Michael J. Smith, Francis R. Scobee, and Ronald E. McNair. This was the first NASA flight with a civilian aboard.

Testing Space Shuttles

The space race with the Soviet Union was on, and the United States was winning. The first 25 years of the U.S. space program were marked with extraordinary success. Between 1961 and 1986, the National Aeronautics and Space Administration (NASA) had worked miracles, turning predictions into headlines. NASA placed satellites in orbit around the earth that enhanced communications and weather tracking. NASA sent up manned spacecraft to circle the globe. In 1969, NASA placed the first astronaut on the moon. And while rockets explored other planets, NASA laid plans for a space station with a permanent crew. The U.S. space shuttle was a part of that plan.

A Reusable Spacecraft The space shuttle was designed to replace the expendable booster rockets used to launch satellites. Rockets would be used to launch the shuttle into orbit.

Then, after completing its mission, the shuttle would glide to earth and land on a runway like an airplane.

After a decade of development and testing, NASA launched the first of several shuttles into orbit on April 12, 1981. It landed two days later at Edwards Air Force Base in California. Twenty-three successful flights followed. The shuttle seemed as reliable as a public bus. In fact, the shuttle was deemed so safe that on its 25th mission, it was to carry a civilian—Christa McAuliffe, a high school teacher from New Hampshire. As part of the Teacher-in-Space Program, Christa McAuliffe was to broadcast two science lessons from the shuttle to millions of students around the country.

Questions of Safety With the exception of the fire on the *Apollo 1* launching pad, which killed three astronauts in 1967, NASA's safety record was excellent. Some NASA

supervisors, however, knew of potential problems with the booster rockets' O-rings. These rubber seals were designed to keep hot gases, which were generated during takeoff, away from the spacecraft's fuel tanks. However, the seals could fail in cold weather. Based on this knowledge, engineers at Morton-Thiokol (the company that manufactured the O-rings) advised postponement of the *Challenger* launch. NASA officials, attempting to keep to a tight schedule, opposed postponement. Morton-Thiokol's top management dropped their objections to the launch in order to accommodate NASA. The fateful launch was approved. Hundreds of special guests had been invited to witness the launch. The guest list included educators, corporate executives, and a delegation from the People's Republic of China.

Seventy-three Seconds

On the cold, crisp morning of January 28, 1986, six crew members and a high school teacher waved triumphantly to the huge crowd before boarding the shuttle *Challenger.* Ice on the shuttle and launching pad delayed a launch that had already been postponed four times. Finally, at 11:38 A.M., the countdown ended, and *Challenger* rose into the sky on a pillar of fire and smoke. The crowd cheered.

Against the clear blue background, the shuttle rocketed into space at 2,900 feet per second. In just over a minute, it was 50,800 feet high and 7 nautical miles from the launch site. Suddenly the onlookers gasped. Just 73 seconds after liftoff, *Challenger* exploded in a ball of flame. The crowd, which included many of the crew's family members and friends, watched in horror as the shuttle appeared to evaporate. Across the nation, television viewers sat in stunned silence.

Earlier shuttle flights had damaged the O-rings. In the cold weather and strong winds of January 28, the predicted possible failure occurred. Superhot gases reached the main fuel tank, which in turn ignited. *Challenger* burned explosively. The horrified crowd watched with a small measure of hope as a lone parachute—part of a booster rocket's descent system—drifted slowly down to sea. Most spectators did not know that the crew had no way to escape during the launch sequence. All seven aboard died instantly.

For more than an hour after the explosion, debris rained from the sky. This created much difficulty for recovery teams working in the area. The shuttle's solid rocket boosters, which are normally recovered for future use, broke away from the craft. The Air Force triggered the boosters' self-destruct mechanism before they could fall to earth, causing further catastrophe. One booster rocket, burning at 5,600° F., had been headed for New Smyrna Beach, a coastal community in Florida, and could have caused much destruction and possibly deaths.

Immediate Suspension

NASA suspended all shuttle flights until a commission appointed by President Ronald Reagan could investigate the accident. The commission found that the problem was much deeper than just the faulty O-ring seals. The commission blamed NASA mid-level supervisors for not telling their superiors about the O-ring problems. The commission also claimed that the space agency was negligent in regard to safety precautions and quality control. Safety issues, such as the O-ring seals, had been pushed aside to meet the pressures of an "overambitious" launch schedule. President Reagan said that the accident was due to the "carelessness that grew out of success." The commission recommended that NASA restructure its management and make safety modifications to the shuttle.

Shuttle flights resumed in September 1988 with the launch of *Discovery.* More than 40 successful shuttle missions have occurred since. Recent shuttle flights focused on retrieving a stray communications satellite and conducting experiments in space.

◀ Despite several earlier delays, the *Challenger* launch seemed routine.

▲ Seconds after the launch, these smoke clouds were all that was visible.

Nuclear
Explosion
at Chernobyl

An explosion at a Soviet nuclear
reactor was the most serious
nuclear accident in history.

A New Nuclear City

As a major industrial power, the former Soviet Union consumed great amounts of electricity and needed to find new sources of energy. In the early 1980s, the government built a nuclear-generated power plant with four reactors in the Ukraine, about 10 miles from the town of Chernobyl and 80 miles from the city of Kiev. The government also built the town of Pripyat, near the power plant, to house the workers and their families.

In nuclear plants, uranium atoms are split to produce heat. The heat is used to boil water, producing steam, which is then used to power generators. Radiation is also produced during this process. Nuclear radiation is dangerous to health. To control it, nuclear facilities have numerous safety features. The four powerful reactors at Chernobyl, however, were built using outdated designs. They lacked some of the improved safety features that reactors in other nations had. For example, the reactors lacked containment structures, which limit the spread of radiation in case of an accident.

Disaster Strikes

On April 25, 1986, workers at the Chernobyl plant tested the reactor. They turned off the plant's emergency cooling system and blocked other automatic safety systems so they wouldn't interfere with the test. When the power level dropped dangerously low during the test, workers tried to generate more energy. They removed most of the rods used to control the level of energy generated at the reactor's core.

At about 1:00 A.M. on April 26, steam started to increase the pressure inside one of the reactors. Operators ignored the warning lights indicating that the reactor should be shut down immediately. About 20 minutes later, the core started to overheat as the nuclear reaction went out of control. The power surge shattered the nuclear fuel. Operators tried to turn on the safety systems but failed. Within seconds, two explosions blew the roof off reactor no. 4. A third explosion ignited 30 fires around the plant. The fire inside the reactor burned at a superhot 2,800° F.

A Strange Glow The explosions forced glowing, radioactive debris high into the air. Witnesses reported seeing an unearthly blue glow coming from the direction of the plant. The reactor was giving off more radiation than the atomic bombs dropped on Hiroshima and Nagasaki in 1945. Workers rushed over from other spots in the plant to see what had happened. Emergency crews got to work immediately to try to put out fires before the flames could reach the other reactors. But in a short time, they had received large doses of radiation. When they were taken away to be treated for radiation poisoning, new crews moved in. Firefighters could not get close enough to the reactor to extinguish the fire. Instead, they smothered it by dumping boron, lead, and sand on it from helicopters. It took 5,000 tons of these materials and nearly two weeks to extinguish the flames.

Immediately following the accident, helicopters sprayed decontaminants over the region.

Officials used current photographs to track the long-term effects of radiation on the people who lived and worked in the area.

Follow-up studies of the radioactivity in the area were made to determine when people will be able to return to their homes.

The High Cost of Power

Damage Control The world learned of the disaster when radioactive dust fell from the sky in Sweden. It also fell over the western half of the Soviet Union and over parts of Europe. At first, the Soviet government denied that anything had happened. When it finally did admit that the accident occurred, it provided few details. Rumors flew—of many deaths and mass graves. It was later revealed that 31 people were killed and 500 injured following the explosion. About 135,000 people living within 20 miles of the plant were evacuated. Yielding to pressure from the West, Soviet leaders finally admitted that the accident was the result of "gross violations of operating regulations by the workers." Several plant officials were arrested and convicted of safety violations.

In the weeks following the accident, the Soviets built a 300,000-ton concrete tomb around the damaged reactor to prevent more radiation leaks. They removed contaminated topsoil and trees and buried them. They drilled new wells to avoid using contaminated water. Buildings were scrubbed to remove radioactive dust. But the plant and the surrounding area were already poisoned.

Future Risks The area is still too radioactive to allow people to return to their homes. A ghostly silence has fallen around Chernobyl. Contaminated areas may not be habitable for decades, if ever. Health experts expect to see increased cancer rates in the region. Already the rate of thyroid cancer in children who were downwind of the power plant is many times higher than normal. It has risen from about 4 cases a year to 60. Thousands of people are expected to get some form of cancer, and many will die of the disease. It is too soon to tell how far-reaching the effects of the Chernobyl accident will be. However, the explosion provided strong new arguments for those who oppose nuclear power.

The *Exxon Valdez* Oil Spill

The grounding of an oil tanker off Alaska caused the largest oil disaster in U.S. history.

The Alaska Pipeline

In 1968, U.S. oil companies struck gold—black gold. Beneath Alaska's North Slope, they found the largest deposit of oil in the United States. A group of oil companies formed a company, called the Alyeska Pipeline Service Company, to build and manage a pipeline to pump the oil across the state to the sea. The trans-Alaska pipeline was completed in 1977. Almost immediately, conflict arose between the oil companies and environmentalists, who were afraid of what oil development might do to Alaska's unique ecosystem. Environmentalists warned that an oil spill at the pipeline's end in Prince William Sound would be disastrous. Such a spill would seriously hurt the fishing industry—a major segment of Alaska's economy. A spill would also harm the area's bird and marine life. In response to the environmentalists' concerns, Alyeska developed plans to deal with any spill that might occur. The next 12 years passed without a mishap.

The Shipwreck

The oil tanker *Exxon Valdez* left the pipeline terminal at Valdez, Alaska, around 9:30 P.M. on Thursday, March 23, 1989. With a cargo of 53 million gallons of oil, the supertanker headed for Long Beach, California. A light snow was falling, and icebergs from the Columbia Glacier drifted into the shipping lane. Captain Joseph Hazelwood, who had been drinking at the time, turned the vessel over to an inexperienced third mate and retired to his cabin. In order to avoid the icebergs, the mate steered the *Exxon Valdez* out of its shipping lane.

At four minutes past midnight, the *Valdez* crew felt the ship collide with the submerged rocks of Bligh Reef. The impact made huge gashes in the tanker's steel hull, pouring millions of gallons of oil into the sound. The ship could not move. The crew immediately began to assess the damage. Twenty minutes later, Captain Hazelwood called the Coast Guard and told them that the *Exxon Valdez* had run aground and was leaking oil.

Plans Gone Wrong The cleanup effort began, but it started late and was disorganized. In its emergency plans, Alyeska had promised to have cleanup crews in action within five

Booms, which are floating barriers, were placed around the tanker to contain the surface oil. But they had arrived too late; the oil had already begun to spread.

The oil slick at Rocky Point was a nightmare for the area's fishing industry.

hours of a spill. But it took the first crews more than ten hours to arrive after the tanker hit the reef.

Other problems plagued the cleanup. Because the cleanup equipment had not been used for many years, much of it was in storage or in need of repair. Cleanup crews counted on using chemicals to dissolve the oil, but the weather was too calm. These chemicals need wave action to work, as detergents need motion in a washing machine. After three days the wind did pick up—but too much. It became too windy to fly the planes that sprayed the chemicals. Moreover, the water was too rough to use boats.

Cleanup workers seemed helpless to stop the spread of the shiny black oil. Within a week it covered 900 square miles—about three-quarters the area of Rhode Island. The natural movement of the tides carried the oil to shore. Eventually oil coated 1,000 miles of shoreline.

Steam cleaning, an environmentally safe cleanup method, was used on the beaches along Prince William Sound.

Environmental Impact

The *Exxon Valdez* oil spill caused enormous destruction of marine and animal life in Prince William Sound. Fur and feathers lose their ability to keep animals and birds warm when coated with oil. Sea otters, gulls, geese, loons, and ducks froze to death. Birds drowned because they could neither float nor fly with the oil on their feathers. Otters ate the oil-covered plants and were poisoned. Bald eagles ate dead birds on the shore. They, too, were poisoned.

The U.S. Fish and Wildlife Service counted about 30,000 dead birds and more than 1,000 dead sea otters. They believe that many more died and sank to the bottom before being counted. Volunteers tried to clean the birds and otters, but they were unable to save more than a few.

The spill hurt fish and the fish industry as well. Fishing fleets could not take herring, salmon, crab, or other seafood from the contaminated areas. On shore, crews tried to clean the beaches. They could remove only some of the oil that lay on the surface. Much of it had seeped into the sand.

Closing the Barn Door After the spill, the Alaskan government passed stricter new laws to ensure prompt cleanup of spills. The state government sued Exxon for the huge cost of the cleanup. And the federal government sued the company for allowing an inexperienced crew member to command the ship. Captain Hazelwood was found not guilty of negligent oil discharge because he had reported the spill to the Coast Guard. He was also found not guilty of operating the ship under the influence of alcohol. Exxon, however, fired him.

The greatest impact of this oil spill may be that it gave environmentalists strong new arguments to use against oil development in ecologically sensitive areas.

Local residents had many reasons to be angry: emergency equipment arrived too late, and there was too little of it.

The Death of the Aral Sea

The diversion of river water for irrigation drastically reduced the size of a gigantic inland sea.

A Great Salt Lake

The Aral Sea was a large saltwater lake between Kazakhstan and Uzbekistan in the former Soviet Union. This desert lake was formed about 1.6 million years ago, when a large depression in the earth's crust filled with water. The Aral Sea became the world's fourth largest inland body of water—bigger than Lake Huron or Lake Michigan. It covered about 26,300 square miles.

The lake is fed by two rivers. The Syr Darya flows into the Aral Sea's northeast corner. The Amu Darya pours into the lake from the south. Because the area around the lake receives only about four inches of rainfall a year, it relies on the two rivers to fill it. Because the water evaporates in hot weather, the lake has a high salt and mineral content. Still, it supported large populations of fish. Towns on the lake's shores were important fishing ports.

Cotton Is King

The former Soviet Union was one of the world's leading cotton producers. In the 1960s, cotton farming was the most important industry in Uzbekistan. Cotton plants need huge amounts of water to thrive. Producing a single bale of cotton takes 105,000 gallons of water. In attempting to increase cotton production, the Soviet government tapped the Syr Darya and Amu Darya to provide more water for the crop. The rivers shrank in size. The Amu Darya, once more than a quarter mile wide, was reduced to a few streams of 50 or 60 yards. By the 1980s, water levels of the rivers were so low that they did not reach the lake at all in the dry summer season.

The water in the sea itself evaporated at a faster rate than the exhausted rivers could fill it. Soon the Aral Sea began to shrink. Between 1960 and 1990, it lost about 40 percent of its surface area. It covered only 15,800 square miles. The level of the lake dropped about 40 feet. The port of Aralsk, once on the lake's northeast shore, now sits more than 40 miles from the water.

As the sea decreased in size, the salt and mineral content of the water increased. As a result, 20 of the 24 native fish species disappeared, and many animals died from drinking the seawater.

As the waters receded, many large salt and mineral deposits were left on the dried bottom. Each year, about 47 million tons of these deposits are blown onto the surrounding lands and carried by rain to vast stretches of nearby areas. They are highly toxic to many plants. Little or nothing grows on the former lake floor.

To provide water for the growing cotton plants, the government diverted water from the two rivers that fed the Aral Sea.

As the Aral Sea evaporated, the areas surrounding it became ghost towns.

Facing Changes

Life Changes Draining the rivers that fed the lake changed the Aral Sea basin in many ways.

- Loss of so many fish species put an end to the region's fishing industry. The fish that remained were poisoned by pesticides, making them harmful to eat.

- People in the area feared eating vegetables grown in the region's contaminated soil.

- As animals in the region died, the hunting and trapping industry collapsed.

- The desert that surrounded the lake is spreading rapidly.

- Safe drinking water became scarce.

- The decline in the quality of drinking water led to higher rates of intestinal illness and throat cancer. The area's infant mortality rate is one of the highest in the world.

Climate Changes The climate of the region had changed, too. Large bodies of water like the Aral Sea help moderate climate. Today in the Aral Sea basin, summers are hotter and winters are colder. Because the growing season is shorter and drier, many cotton farmers have switched to other crops. The people of Uzbekistan are angry about the changes to their environment. The government is studying possible solutions. More efficient irrigation systems would lower the amount of water drawn from the rivers. Irrigation drainage could be directed back to the lake. Farmers could grow crops that need less water than cotton. A canal could be built to bring water from the Irtysh River, which is 800 miles away, to the Aral Sea. But these solutions would take time to implement—and might create problems of their own.

Environmentalists throughout the world are increasingly concerned about how natural resources are used. Environmental education begins early as these Hong Kong children celebrate Earth Day.

The Gulf War Oil Disaster

Ecological ruin followed the Persian Gulf War.

Hussein Invades Neighbor

In the summer of 1990, Saddam Hussein, the president of Iraq, accused Kuwait of plotting with the United States to keep oil prices low. Hussein needed oil revenues to help rebuild his country after its long war with Iran. Hussein claimed that oil fields along the border of Iraq and Kuwait and two strategically located islands in the Persian Gulf belonged to Iraq. On August 1, representatives from the two countries met to discuss their differences. Nothing was resolved. The next day, Iraqi tanks and troops crossed the border into Kuwait. The world was stunned by the invasion.

Desert Storm Despite world pressure, Hussein would not withdraw. The possibility of war became very real. Environmentalists were concerned that a war would harm the environment. In 1983, Iraq had bombed Iranian offshore oil platforms, spilling two million barrels of oil into the Persian Gulf. This time, the potential for destruction was greater.

Ecoterrorism

On January 16, 1991, an American-led coalition of armies launched air and missile attacks against Iraq and Iraqi-occupied Kuwait. In the weeks that followed, huge amounts of oil spilled into the gulf. Iraqis opened pumps at a supertanker loading dock. For several days oil leaked into the gulf at a rate of about four million gallons a day. After a week, the resulting slick covered 350 square miles. Another three million gallons of petroleum poured into the gulf when Iraqis emptied the oil from five fully loaded tankers into the water. Eventually the oil covered 400 miles of beaches in Saudi Arabia with a layer of oil a foot thick. On January 22, Iraqis set fire to Kuwait's Wafra oil field. To prevent counterattack, they dug miles of trenches along the beach and filled them with oil. U.S. President George Bush believed that these acts of environmental terrorism were a "last gasp" measure. But the Iraqis were not yet finished.

Desperate Measures On February 21, in the final days of the Gulf War, Iraqi troops began destroying Kuwait's oil installations. They set fire to about 800 of more than 1,000 oil wells. The burning wells consumed about six million barrels a day, valued at about $110 million. The effects were dramatic:

- Day turned to night as thick black clouds blocked all sunlight.

- In smoky areas, temperatures were as much as 18 degrees below normal.

- The black smoke and soot contained carbon monoxide and sulfur dioxide that caused breathing problems over hundreds of miles.

- Sulfur dioxide made paint peel and metal corrode.

- Fallout from the fire covered the desert with a layer of tar.

- Oil wells that weren't burning leaked enough petroleum to create huge oil lakes, which threatened to burst into flame.

Countries in the gulf region watched in fear as Saddam Hussein ordered the invasion of Kuwait and, later, the destruction of the oil fields.

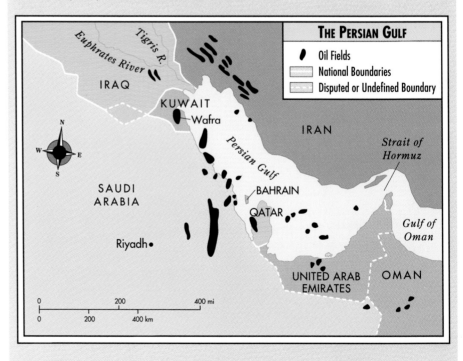

A shepherd tends his flock near the burning oil fields outside Kuwait City. The fires posed a serious health threat to all who lived in the region.

In some places seawater was used to control the fires. However, it took many months to finally extinguish all the fires.

After the War

Slow Progress The war ended on March 6, 1991, with the defeat of Hussein's forces and their expulsion from Kuwait. The cleanup of the oil spills and the extinguishing of the fires began immediately. But the plans for the cleanup did not realistically reflect the scope of the disaster. Floating booms used to collect oil on top of the water had to be flown in from Alaska. Money and equipment were slow to arrive. For each day of delay, another 3,000 barrels of oil drained into the gulf. The cleanup was also hampered by the remnants of war. Unexploded mines that surrounded burning oil wells had to be disarmed before firefighting teams could move in.

By July 4, teams had cleaned up most of the floating oil, but great damage had been done. The Persian Gulf is a shallow and contained body of water. Unlike open ocean, it does not renew itself quickly. The spill had a severe impact on the fish and shrimp industries. Sensitive ecosystems—swamps, coral reefs, and sea grass beds—were contaminated. Sea turtles and porpoises were affected. An estimated 25,000 grebes, cormorants, and other birds died as a result of the oil spills. Many birds died trying to drink from ponds of oil.

Black Rain The last of the oil well fires was put out on November 6— sooner than expected. But by then, soot covered 75 percent of Kuwait's desert, and black, oily rain fell as far away as Turkey and the former Soviet Union. The rain also damaged crops in Iran and Pakistan.

A total of about 600 million barrels of oil, valued at $12 billion, had been lost in the eight-month-long blaze. The firefighting effort had cost an estimated $2 billion.

The devastation in Kuwait was massive. Thousands of seabirds were killed and Saudi Arabia's shrimp industry was seriously threatened. Many environmental activists have pushed for assurances that ecoterrorism would not be used again. One proposal that has been suggested calls for an international agreement to make ecoterrorism a punishable crime.

Hurricanes Andrew and Iniki

Within weeks of each other, two severe hurricanes battered the United States.

By watching satellite photos, such as this one, meteorologists can make predictions about the intensity and direction of a storm.

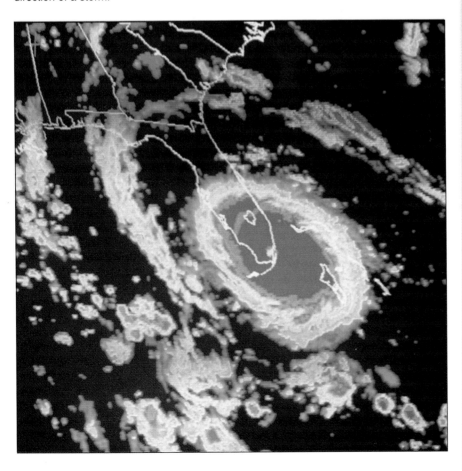

A Hurricane Forms

Hurricanes generally develop in late summer and early fall, when the surface temperatures of tropical oceans reach 80° F. or more. The hot, humid air rises and forms a column of clouds. The surrounding air flows toward this rising column. Because of the earth's rotation, this air starts to spin. As the winds get stronger, the storm is classified as a tropical storm. When the spiraling winds reach 75 miles per hour (mph), the storm's classification changes to a Force 1 hurricane. A Force 5 hurricane, the most severe, has winds greater than 155 mph. A hurricane has an area of calmness at its center, or eye, that is 5 to 20 miles across. Winds in the eye of the hurricane may be only 15 mph. Violent winds and torrential rains surround the eye.

As people were warned about the approaching storm, they took precautions to protect their homes and businesses from potential damage.

The Storms Strike

Andrew At 11:00 P.M. on Sunday, August 23, 1992, Hurricane Andrew ripped across the Bahamas. The storm left four people dead and devastated one island. Four hours later, Andrew slammed into South Florida. Storm-driven waves pounded shore areas. Heavy rainfall contributed to inland flooding. But the worst damage came from the wind. At 145 mph, sometimes gusting to 165 mph, the wind blew out windows, uprooted power lines, and even ripped the weather radar off the National Hurricane Center building. The wind blew down homes and wiped the city of Homestead off the map. Then it turned west across the Gulf of Mexico and destroyed property and crops in Louisiana.

Iniki Three weeks later, on September 11, a hurricane of equal strength hit the island of Kauai, Hawaii. Waves were 20 feet high and winds reached 160 mph. Hurricane Iniki damaged half of the island's 21,000 homes. Eight thousand people were left homeless and 2,000 vacationers were stranded on the island when the storm hit.

Picking Up the Pieces

Andrew's Damage Hurricane Andrew killed 39 people in the Bahamas, Florida, and Louisiana, and left 300,000 people homeless. In Florida alone, 85,000 homes were damaged or destroyed. The path of destruction through South Florida was 20 to 35 miles wide. Some said it looked as though an atomic bomb had been dropped. Entire neighborhoods were flattened and left without any recognizable landmarks.

People were uprooted by the devastation:

- The newly homeless sought shelter in makeshift tent cities.
- Parts of Florida and Louisiana were left without power or water.
- Telephone service was cut off.
- Lack of sewage treatment raised concern about the spread of diseases such as cholera.

Temporary medical clinics were established in any building still standing—including a local motel. The air was filled with the foul odor of spoiled food and dead house pets rotting in the blistering tropical heat. Damage estimates ranged as high as $30 billion, making Hurricane Andrew the most expensive storm in history.

Iniki's Aftermath Similar to South Florida, Kauai lost power and water. Restoring electricity to the entire island took several months. For days the airport was closed and transportation unavailable. Sand filled the lower floors of luxury hotels. Damage to crops was severe. Acres of sugarcane and other crops were destroyed. Some speculated that the storm damage might be enough to kill the island's struggling sugarcane industry.

Too Little, Too Late? It took several days for the government agency in charge of relief efforts to provide storm victims with food, water, and shelter. People criticized the Federal Emergency Management Agency (FEMA) for its slow response. Eventually the U.S. government approved $10.5 billion to help rebuild Florida, Louisiana, and Hawaii after the storms. Insurance companies expect to pay nearly $11 billion in claims for property damage.

One reason given to explain why the damage was so great is that buildings weren't constructed in these areas to withstand such high winds. Building too near the coast also contributed to the high rate of damage.

Early Warning The cost in human life might have been much higher if the National Hurricane Center had not been able to warn people in advance. Because of the early warning, many people had been safely evacuated to other areas.

Hurricanes like Andrew and Iniki are expected to strike only once or twice in a century. Some scientists, however, are concerned that severe hurricanes may become more common. Global warming, which is the trend toward higher average temperatures, may strengthen the forces that cause such severe storms. This trend might explain why four Force 5 hurricanes—once called "hundred-year storms"—have ravaged North and Central America since 1988.

Officials estimate that it will take more than $20 billion to repair the damage from hurricanes Andrew and Iniki.

Glossary

active volcano: A volcano that is currently erupting.

AIDS (acquired immune deficiency syndrome): An infectious disease caused by a virus (HIV). By weakening the immune system, AIDS puts people at risk of developing other serious diseases such as pneumonia and cancer. No cure for AIDS is known.

antibiotic: A substance that inhibits the growth of or destroys bacteria and other microorganisms; used to treat certain diseases.

archaeologist: A scientist who studies the cultures of ancient peoples, usually by excavating ruins.

bacterium (pl. bacteria): One of a group of one-celled microorganisms, most of which multiply by cell division. Some bacteria cause disease; others perform useful functions.

bubo: A swollen lymph gland, especially in the armpit or groin.

bubonic plague: A contagious disease caused by a bacterium and characterized by fever, flulike symptoms, and buboes; also called the Black Death. The disease is transmitted by fleas from infected rats.

bucket brigade: A line of persons who pass along buckets of water to put out a fire.

coalition: A temporary alliance of several nations for a specific purpose.

crater: A pit at the mouth of a volcano.

cyclone: A storm with winds that rotate about a center of low atmospheric pressure; the rotation is counterclockwise in the Northern Hemisphere and clockwise in the Southern Hemisphere. Cyclones are often accompanied by heavy rains.

delta: Sediment deposited at the mouth of a river, usually in a triangular shape.

dormant volcano: A volcano that is temporarily inactive.

ecosystem: A community of living things—plants, animals, and microorganisms—and the physical environment they share.

ecoterrorism: Terroristic political activity that harms the environment.

epidemic: An outbreak of disease that spreads rapidly and affects a large part of a population.

fault: A fracture in the earth's crust along which movement has occurred.

firebreak: A strip of cleared land used to fight a fire by depriving it of fuel.

global warming: A trend toward higher average temperatures on earth.

HIV (human immunodeficiency virus): The virus that causes AIDS in humans. HIV can be transmitted through body fluids such as blood and by sexual contact. A person can be infected with HIV for years without developing AIDS.

host: An organism on which a parasite lives or feeds.

hurricane: A violent tropical cyclone with winds of at least 74 mph.

influenza: A highly contagious viral disease whose symptoms include fever, sore throat, and aching muscles; also called flu.

intravenous: Injected into a vein.

lava: Melted rock flowing out of a volcano.

lymph glands: Parts of the lymphatic system in which bacteria and other harmful substances are collected; also called lymph nodes. Lymph glands are located in the neck, armpits, groin, abdomen, and chest.

multinational corporation: A corporation with branches in several countries.

nomadic: Moving from place to place in search of food, with no permanent home.

oceanographer: A scientist who studies the physical features, life-forms, or natural resources of the oceans.

paddy: A flooded field where rice is grown.

pesticide: A substance used to kill pests such as insects or weeds. Pesticides are strong chemicals that can have harmful effects on desirable organisms.

pneumonia: An infection of the lungs caused by either a virus or a bacterium.

potato blight: A serious disease caused by a fungus that destroys potato plants.

pumice: A volcanic rock that is very light and full of holes.

reactor: A device that produces energy by means of nuclear fission.

scrubber: A device for removing impurities from a gas.

smallpox: A highly contagious viral disease characterized by fever and by skin eruptions that often leave permanent scars. Through the use of vaccines, the virus has been eliminated worldwide.

space shuttle: A reusable spacecraft that carries two solid rocket boosters to help lift it into orbit and an external fuel tank that holds liquid fuel. After the shuttle is in orbit, the solid rocket boosters and the fuel tank drop off. When the shuttle returns to earth, it lands on a runway like a plane.

submersible: Capable of operating under water.

tsunami: A giant sea wave caused by an underwater earthquake or volcanic eruption; sometimes called a tidal wave.

tuberculosis: A contagious disease caused by a bacterium and usually affecting the lungs.

vaccine: A substance injected into the body to produce immunity to a disease. A vaccine usually consists of a killed or weakened form of the organism that causes the disease.

virus: One of a group of disease-causing agents that are smaller and simpler than other microorganisms; viruses are capable of reproduction and growth only inside living cells. A viral infection cannot be treated with drugs, but some can be prevented with vaccines.

volcano: A vent in the earth's crust through which gas and molten rock can be expelled.

Suggested Readings

Note: An asterisk (*) denotes a Young Adult title.

The Age of Calamity (1300–1400 AD). Time-Life Books, 1989.

*Anderson, Madelyn K. *Oil in Troubled Waters: Cleaning Up Oil Spills.* Franklin Watts, 1983.

Barrett, Norman. *Hurricanes and Tornadoes.* Franklin Watts, 1990.

Benson, Ragnar. *The Greatest Explosions in History: The Fire, Flash, and Fury of Natural and Man-made Disasters.* Carol Publishing Group, 1993.

*Blashfield, Jean F., and Black, Wallace B. *Oil Spills.* Grolier, 1991.

Cahill, Richard A. *Disasters at Sea:* Titanic *to the* Exxon Valdez. Nautical Books, 1991.

Chaiken, Miriam A. *A Nightmare in History: Holocaust, 1933–1945.* Clarion Books, 1987.

Davis, Lee. *Man-made Catastrophes: From the Burning of Rome to the Lockerbie Crash.* Facts on File, 1992.

———. *Natural Disasters: From the Black Plague to the Eruption of Mt. Pinatubo.* Facts on File, 1992.

Ebert, Charles H. *Disasters: Violence of Nature and Threats by Man.* Kendall-Hunt, 1988.

Ekey, Robert. *Yellowstone on Fire.* Falcon Press, 1989.

Everest, Larry. *Behind the Poison Cloud: Union Carbide's Bhopal Massacre.* Banner Press, 1986.

Great Disasters: Dramatic True Stories of Nature's Awesome Powers. Reader's Digest Association, 1989.

*Hare, Tony. *The Ozone Layer.* Franklin Watts, 1990.

Hawley, T. M. *Against the Fires of Hell: The Ecological Consequences of the Persian Gulf War.* Harcourt Brace Jovanovich, 1992.

Hersey, John. *Hiroshima.* Alfred A. Knopf, 1985.

*Knapp, Brian. *Drought.* Raintree Steck-Vaughn, 1990.

*———. *Earthquake.* Raintree Steck-Vaughn, 1990.

*———. *Fire.* Raintree Steck-Vaughn, 1990.

*———. *Flood.* Raintree Steck-Vaughn, 1990.

*———. *Storm.* Raintree Steck-Vaughn, 1990.

*———. *Volcano.* Raintree Steck-Vaughn, 1990.

*Lord, Walter. *A Night to Remember.* Buccaneer Books, 1991.

*Marsh, Carole. *Washington's (Most Devastating!) Disasters and (Most Calamitous!) Catastrophes!* Gallopade Publishing Group, 1990.

*Nardo, Don. *Krakatoa.* Lucent Books, 1990.

O'Grada, Cormac. *The Great Irish Famine.* Macmillan, 1989.

Potter, Jerry O. *The Sultana Tragedy: America's Greatest Maritime Disaster.* Pelican Publishing Company, 1992.

*Scollins, Richard. *The Fire of London.* Franklin Watts, 1992.

Shea, Cynthia P. *A Vanishing Shield: Protecting the Ozone Layer.* Worldwatch Institute, 1988.

Tufty, Barbara. *One Thousand and One Questions Answered About Earthquakes, Avalanches, Floods, and Other Natural Disasters.* Dover Publications, 1987.

Index